Glimpses of History
in
the San Gorgonio Pass
in the 19th Century

Betty Kikumi Meltzer
and
Louis Philip Doody

Cherry Valley, California

2011

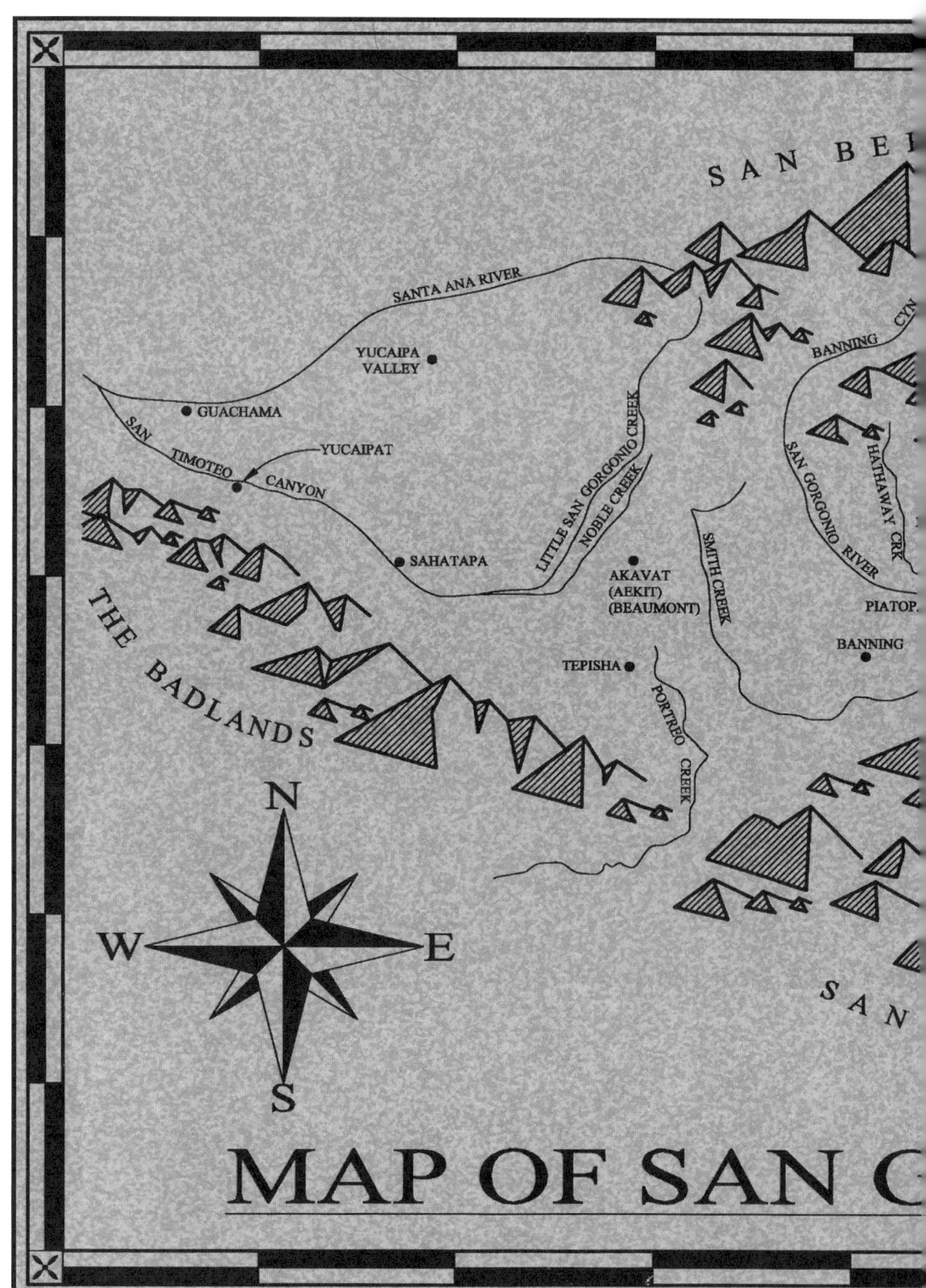

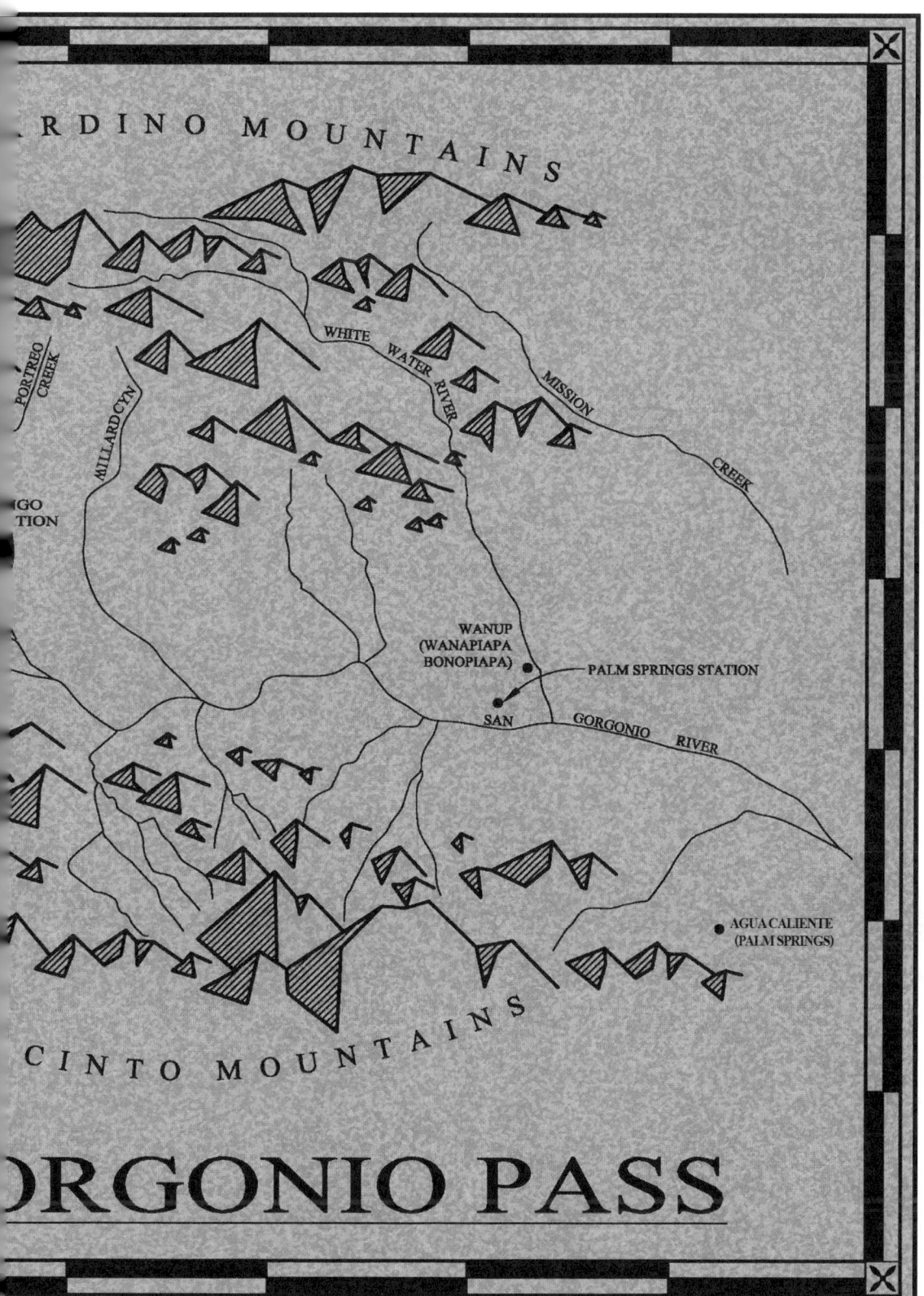

Published by Malki-Ballena Press

Copyright © 2011 by the authors
All Rights Reserved

No part of this book may be reproduced
in any form without written
permission of the copyright owners.

Malki Museum, Inc.
P.O. Box 578
11-795 Fields Road
Banning, CA 92220
951 849-7289 (fax) 951 849-3549
www.malkimuseum.org

ISBN 0-939046-47-4

Meltzer, Betty Kikumi, and Doody, Louis Philip.
1. History—California—San Gorgonio Pass, 1810-1892. 2. Cahuilla people
3. History—California—Spanish and Mexican periods

Book design and composition by Steve Moore
Project Management by Elaine Mathews

Map of the San Gorgonio Pass by Philip M. Doody

About the mural on the cover: The art work on the cover is from a portion of a Works Progress Administration mural that was painted in 1939 by Pauline Hirst and Edwin Frank on the north wall of what was then the Banning High School library. The whole mural depicts the history of San Gorgonio Pass from the time of the Native Americans forward. The right-hand portion of the mural, shown on the front cover depicts Dr. Isaac Smith in the 1850s receiving the deed from Paulino Weaver to the property that is today occupied by the Highland Springs Resort. It may be Weaver's adobe that is depicted behind the two figures. On the left side of the mural a priest is shown ministering to the Cahuilla people. The Cahuilla people of the Pass were on the outermost ranch of a mission network under the authority of the San Gabriel Mission near Los Angeles. As such, they were Mission Indians, though many retained traditional beliefs. The Cahuilla figures are shown carrying their harvest of acorns or other seeds. In the left foreground is a representation of a stagecoach that belonged to the Bradshaw Line that ran from Los Angeles to Arizona in the days of the gold rush. In the Pass, the line ran from Palm Springs to Whitewater, to Gilman Ranch, to Highland Springs, Singleton Road and down through San Timoteo Canyon. The mural is in the national databse of WPA murals and is a piece of federal property presented to the citizens of the area.

Preface

This little book of historic episodes about Southern California's San Gorgonio Pass in the 19th century is intended for two groups: first, young readers, especially those living in or near the Pass, and second, adults who have a general interest in the history of Southern California's native people.

It is based on several years of research first undertaken in 2004. As retired teachers of the Banning Unified School District, we long felt the need for material in the schools that focused on the history of the Cahuilla people of the San Gorgonio Pass whose children attended Banning schools. In the course of our research we came to realize that the San Gorgonio Pass and its history really encompass the twenty-five mile or so area from the city of Redlands at the northwest entrance of the Pass to the southeastern entrance of the Pass near Whitewater. Thus, the booklet would have significance for students in the school districts of Redlands, Loma Linda, Yucaipa, Calimesa, Beaumont, Banning, Whitewater, and very likely the larger nearby cities of Riverside, San Bernardino, Colton and Palm Springs because the Cahuilla nation once extended throughout this region and beyond. We feel that the book partly fills a gap in our knowledge because it places the local history of Banning and Beaumont in a broader geographical context and because it goes back to a time preceding the arrival of American settlers in the region.

In some respects, this book also represents a condensation of our longer and more scholarly treatment of the history of the Cahuilla people in this period entitled *Losing Ground: The Displacement of San Gorgonio Pass Cahuilla People in the 19th Century*. The serious student of history will find a fuller treatment of events as well as a lengthy bibliography and interesting material in the appendices of that book.

All five chapters of this booklet relate in some manner to the theme of the displacement of the Cahuilla people from their homelands in the nineteenth century. In such little space it cannot aim to discuss the rich culture of the Cahuilla people. There is a diversity of books on this subject already in print, especially the excellent titles offered by the Malki-Ballena Press at the Morongo Reservation.

Our booklet will shed light on what happened to the Pass Cahuilla people under the rule of Spain, a relatively short period of time from 1819 when the San Bernardino outpost was established at Guachama to 1821; under the Mexican government from 1821 to approximately 1848; and last, under the Americans from 1848 to 1892.

Readers will discover amazing things about Pass history during those years, in addition to facts that are generally unknown or often ignored. For instance, who realized that today's sizeable community of Yucaipa had its humble origins in the lower end of San Timoteo Canyon; that the Cahuilla people were the ones who built the structures, created irrigation ditches, planted orchards and fields and tended the vast herds of cattle that were introduced in this area; that over a thousand Cahuillas gathered for meetings in the 1850s near today's Highland Springs Resort in Cherry Valley; that a Cahuilla leader, Juan Antonio, and his followers annihilated an outlaw gang from Los Angeles that included some rowdy Australians called the "Sydney ducks"; that Juan del Carmen Lugo, owner of the vast San Bernardino Rancho literally lost his pants in that incident; that Juan Antonio not only overawed Los Angeles, but also caused anxiety in far-away San Francisco; that a half-Cherokee, half-white scout and friend of Kit Carson, Paulino Weaver, became the "first citizen" of Prescott, Arizona after creating havoc in the San Gorgonio Pass for the Cahuilla people; that the U.S. government negotiator, Oliver Wozencraft, presented a treaty that promised all the land from the San Gorgonio Pass to Temecula as a reservation for the Cahuillas, Luiseños and Cocomaricopas and that the U.S. Senate later refused to ratify the treaty, and furthermore, "lost" it for fifty years; that white squatters in the Pass ignored executive orders by Presidents Grant, Garfield and Hayes and settled on land set aside specifically for the Cahuilla people; that Helen Hunt Jackson wrote *Ramona* to focus the nation's attention on the plight of Southern California Indians, including the Cahuillas; that Cahuilla Indians were entitled to their traditional lands and streams under the Treaty of Guadalupe Hidalgo and that a lawsuit brought against them by two white speculators in the 1880s argued against that protection?

We invite you now to explore these aspects of our local history in this booklet and to probe more deeply in the companion volume, *Losing Ground*.

> Betty Kikumi Meltzer, Cherry Valley, California
> Louis Philip Doody, Hilo, Hawaii
> 2011

A section of the zanja dug in 1819 by the Cahuilla Indians of the village of Guachama. It stretched twelve miles from Mill Creek to the Asistencia. This section is found on the campus of the University of Redlands.

Table of Contents

Chapter 1
Solano and the *Zanja* 1

Chapter 2
Paulino Weaver and the Cahuillas 7

Chapter 3
Juan Antonio and the Irving Gang 14

Chapter 4
Juan Antonio and the Treaty of Temecula 18

Chapter 5
The Case of *John Morongo et al vs. John North et al* 23

1

Solano and the Zanja

In 1819 the people of a *rancheria*[1] located in the city today known as Redlands, California, invited Spanish padres to venture forth from San Gabriel Mission near Los Angeles to build an outlying mission station in the San Bernardino Valley.

Guachama was the name of that little *rancheria* and it was located on the south bank of the Santa Ana River, in the western part of Redlands, near Loma Linda and the entrance to San Timoteo Canyon. It is believed that several hundred Cahuilla and Serrano people lived at the village that stretched for two miles along the river. Cahuillas probably outnumbered Serranos in the *rancheria*. The village leader was a man named Solano. He was most likely the one who welcomed the men sent out from San Gabriel to design structures and a water supply system for the mission.

Sources say that the padres of Mission San Gabriel had established an earlier station in the San Bernardino Valley at Politana, in present-day Colton, as early as 1810, but that people there who opposed the mission attacked and destroyed it. Survivors of that attack may have been the same people who called for the padres to establish a new mission outpost at Guachama only seven miles east of Politana.

The padres accepted the invitation and sent Carlos Garcia out to be the administrator at Guachama. He was in charge of directing the construction of a chapel, a building that would contain storerooms for the harvests and a home for the *majordomo,* or manager, to live in. They also sent a man named

---

[1] The word "*rancheria*" refers to an Indian village. This village was located along the south side of the Santa Ana River, not far from where San Timoteo Creek emerges from its canyon. The village of Guachama and the area around it soon became known as San Bernardino.

Chapter 1–Solano and the Zanja

Pedro Alvarez to plan a very important task, the digging of an irrigation ditch that would supply the mission with water for its needs.

The San Gabriel Mission in 1819 was one of twenty-one missions that the Franciscan padres had built in a long line several miles inland, stretching all the way from San Diego in southern California to Sonoma far to the north, beyond San Francisco. Spanish authorities were trying desperately to strengthen Spain's control over California in the late 1700s and early 1800s, afraid that other nations like Russia and England would intrude upon their claim to California. Sending Spanish settlers and soldiers as well as missionaries to work among the Indians, they hoped, were ways to gain firm control of the region.

San Gabriel Mission was among the first four missions that were founded in California. From its beginnings around 1770, it grew into a large and wealthy mission that eventually supported dozens of *ranchos* for raising cattle, horses, pigs, and goats. The padres also introduced important new crops on the *ranchos* like barley, wheat, peas and beans. They planted olive orchards and vineyards as well, using the labor of Indians that they converted to Christianity.

It was about fifty years after the founding of San Gabriel Mission that the first permanent Spanish structure in the San Bernardino Valley was built at the *ranchería* of Guachama. As they almost always did, Spanish and Mexican managers relied upon the labor of the village people to accomplish most of the heavy work. Pedro Alvarez must have worked closely with Solano, the leader of the people of Guachama, to organize his people into a work crew to dig the all-important *zanja* or irrigation ditch. It was a very large and difficult project.

The effort to bring water from Mill Creek, twelve miles away, across the hills and plains, to fields near Guachama required scores if not hundreds of people to accomplish, using the simplest of tools. The project began in 1819 with the damming of the stream at Mill Creek, at present-day Mentone, in order to raise the level of water enough to allow it to flow downhill to the mission station. We can imagine the challenges that Solano and his people encountered when carrying out Alvarez' instructions.

The villagers toiled throughout 1819 under hot summer temperatures that rose as high as 110 degrees at times. Scattered native sycamores and elder trees provided scant shade as adult men and women worked, digging and removing soil, gravel and rock, using the scapulas, or shoulder-blades, of cattle as shovels. It must have been discouraging when scapulas cracked or were split from hitting a rock. Not only was the *zanja* long, it was also wide and deep and full of rocky rubble. In some places where the *zanja* passes through the campus of today's University of Redlands, it measures ten feet deep and over fifteen feet across.

Women worked alongside men, moving dirt in baskets on their heads.

Chapter 1–Solano and the Zanja

The villagers tamped down the earth to form an embankment with the soil they piled on the sides of the wide ditch. The boys of the village were luckier than their parents. While the elders worked, the boys snared rabbits and hunted for quail and other small game.

In planning the *zanja*, Alvarez and Solano must have had to walk every foot of the ditch's flow a number of times, following natural contours whenever possible, to minimize the amount of soil that would have to be moved. Eventually, Alvarez figured out the easiest route that would get the water from Mill Creek through the hills (of today's Crafton), but it was impossible to avoid heavy digging when small hills or rises got in the way on the *zanja*'s way to Guachama.

The workers cleared brush all the way along the course of the irrigation ditch. The *zanja* zigzagged around hills and through gullies, wending its way through what is now the University of Redlands campus' south end, through present-day Sylvan Park, down a few miles, where it turned south about half a mile and turned westward. It then hit the plain where the people had prepared agricultural fields. Brush and chapparal were cleared away to make way for the new crops of grain and vegetables, orchards and vineyards.

While some villagers worked on the *zanja* and cleared the fields, other laborers built the mission's chapel, storage room building, and the home for Carlos Garcia, the *majordomo*. Some of the men of the *rancheria* were selected for training to be *vaqueros* (cowboys) to tend the newly-arrived cattle. In time, these few cattle would multiply into large herds roaming the rich San Bernardino grazing grounds. The people of Guachama must have returned to their brush and reed homes very tired at the end of their work days.

Their efforts paid off handsomely and quickly, however. By May, 1820 the work on the *zanja* was finished and it was time to plant the crops.

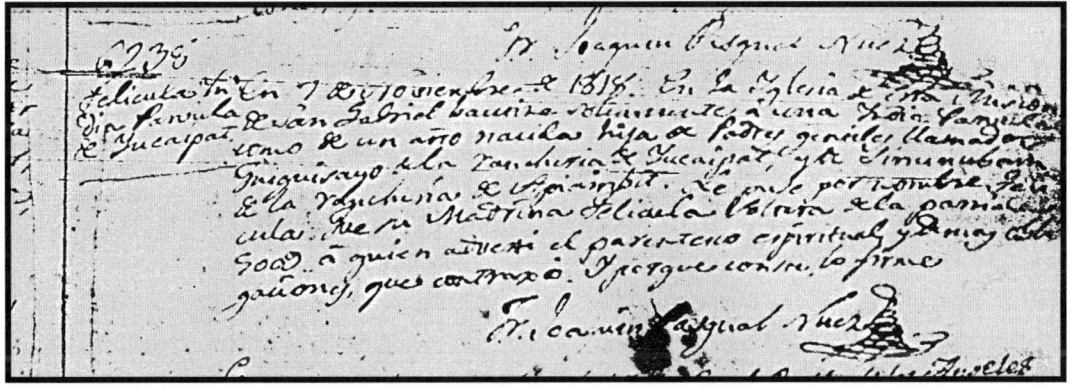

A page showing a baptismal record (#6238) in 1818 of a child from "Yucaipat," which in those days was located in the San Timoteo Canyon. The baptism took place at San Gabriel Mission near Los Angeles. It shows that Spanish influence had spread far inland even before the founding of the Asistencia at Guachama. (LDS Family History Center)

Chapter 1 – Solano and the Zanja

Invitations were issued to Indian villagers living at Jurupa (a *rancheria* a few miles to the west), Serranos in the San Bernardino Mountains and Cahuillas in the San Gorgonio Pass to come and watch the planting of the crops for the first time on what had once been dry, barren ground. Water gushed from the *zanja* into the smaller irrigation channels that ran through the fields and, within months, hundreds of villagers were celebrating their first harvest of beans, corn, peas, and barley. They even had a mill to grind their wheat into flour.

In September of the following year, two visiting padres, Father Payeras, the general manager of the California missions, and Jose Sanchez, his secretary, somehow found their way from San Diego into the back country and down through San Timoteo Canyon to Guachama. By then, the padres of San Gabriel had given the new mission at Guachama a new name: San Bernardino. The two visitors must have been pleasantly surprised to see how much work the Cahuillas and Serranos of the village had accomplished. After exploring the surrounding country for a few more days, they returned to San Bernardino before heading for San Gabriel Mission.

Within a short time, the Indians at San Bernardino were so successful in agriculture that they were able to provide not only for their own needs, but also for visitors who passed through the area. The famous American explorer of the West, Jedediah S. Smith, and his followers, for instance, happened to be in southern California in 1826 when they became desperate for food in order to continue their trek. The padres at San Gabriel Mission had told them that, on their return trip inland, they should stop at the San Bernardino station to secure free supplies. Smith's group followed that advice. They were grateful and relieved to receive corn, peas, parched meal and wheat flour produced by the Cahuillas and Serranos. Without this aid, the expedition would have ended in disaster.

The mission station at San Bernardino in time became known as the Asistencia. This means that the mission engaged in almost the same activities as the main mission at San Gabriel. It provided religious instruction and services for the people of the *rancheria*. It also taught them necessary skills in basic construction, agriculture and cattle-raising in addition to making adobe bricks, working leather and candle-making.

The San Gabriel Mission near Los Angeles, founded a half-century earlier, however, was larger and more important than its outpost at San Bernardino would ever be. It was, of course, the main headquarters of a sprawling agricultural industry affecting the lives of many thousands of southern California Indians. It also outclassed the Asistencia in another way: there was no priest posted permanently at the Asistencia. There were too few priests to serve the large southern California region, so priests came only occasionally to work among the Indians at Guachama. (Even before the

Chapter 1–Solano and the Zanja

Asistencia at San Bernardino had been built, it appears that Cahuilla people from farther inland trekked all the way to San Gabriel for their baptisms.)

Even so, the San Bernardino Asistencia, on its own, grew so large and prosperous that the padres started to consider plans to make it part of a second line of missions from southern to northern California, further inland, following the example of the first string of missions near the Pacific Coast. Its cattle-raising enterprise was so successful that after 1820 the ranch managers had to ride inland, up the San Timoteo Canyon to the summit of today's San Gorgonio Pass to look for more Cahuilla people to work on the ranch. Furthermore, soon after the founding of the Asistencia, there were already two new cattle ranches operating yet further inland. Only a few miles into the San Timoteo Canyon, at the small *rancheria* of Yucaipa,[2] villagers began to raise cattle. About seventeen miles up the canyon from the Asistencia, at the summit of the San Gorgonio Pass, another ranching operation sprang up. It seems to have been headquartered at the village of Piatopa in what is now the Banning Water Canyon. Cattle were already present at the eastern end of the San Gorgonio Pass a few years later, judging from the records of a Mexican exploratory expedition that passed through. There was also an adobe building that possibly dated back to the 1820s or 1830s, in today's Cherry Valley, that may have served as the home for the *majordomo* of the San Gorgonio Rancho.[3] The Asistencia had a definite impact on the Cahuilla people throughout the San Gorgonio Pass.

The success of the Asistencia was not to last. The government of Mexico declared its independence from Spain in the 1820s, but struggled to pay its debts and keep the loyalty of its people. As Mexican leaders looked at the large network of ranches and missions that the padres had established in distant California, built with the hard work of converted Indians, they realized that they could use the missions' wealth for their own purposes. They decided to close the missions and turn the ranches over to Mexican families. This process was called "the secularization of the missions" and it occurred from the 1830s through the 1840s. The government in Mexico City proclaimed the Decree of Secularization in 1833 and mission padres lost control of the California missions in 1834.

Though the Mexican government promised to distribute much of the land, tools and livestock of the missions to the Indians, this did not really happen, except in a few cases. Most of the land and mission property was subdivided into large tracts and granted as *ranchos* to influential Mexican families. It was because of the secularization that the Asistencia and all the land of Rancho San Bernardino were granted to the Lugo family in 1842. The Yucaipa Rancho was granted to a cousin of the Lugos. Two men, Paulino

---
[2] The original Yucaipa was located in San Timoteo Canyon, a few miles away from the Redlands Asistencia, at the place where San Timoteo Road and Live Oak Canyon Road meet.
[3] Some locals referred to the structure as "The Franciscan Chapel."

Chapter 1–Solano and the Zanja

California Historical Landmark Number 42 at the Asistencia in Redlands. It marks the second location of early Rancho San Bernardino buildings on a hill that overlooked the *rancheria* of Guachama. Today you will see a 1930s restoration of the buildings, the first Mexican-era structures in the San Bernardino Valley.

Weaver and Isaac Williams, petitioned Governor Pio Pico for a grant to the San Gorgonio Rancho. The Cahuillas did not inherit the lands that the Decree of Secularization of the Mexican government promised them.

Today, if you want to visit the original site of the Asistencia, you will have a difficult time, because there is nothing there to mark its presence. It was located on Mission Road in Redlands. It is far more convenient to visit the second location of the Asistencia which was built in 1830 when Juan Alvarado was the *majordomo* (1826-1834). It is the restored, mission-like structure on the hill nearby on Barton Road in Redlands. By 1834 this second set of Asistencia buildings was also abandoned and was not restored until the 1930s. You should also try to see the portion of the *zanja* that is still visible on the campus of the University of Redlands. If you do, remember Solano and the people of Guachama whose hard labor built the *zanja* and made the early mission at Guachama a success, thereby easing the way for Americans who claimed California for the United States in 1848.

Paulino Weaver and the Cahuillas

From the earliest years of Mexican rule, Americans and other outsiders had been trickling into California, sometimes marrying into established Mexican families, adopting Spanish given names and Catholicism and founding businesses. Typically these were entrepreneurs from New England who arrived on the California coast after a long voyage around the tip of the South American continent. In the 1830s and 1840s other Americans arrived overland as explorers, guides and trappers. Newly-arriving Americans were often eager to acquire large tracts of land like those of the Californios.

To qualify for such grants, Americans had to petition the Mexican governor of California in addition to adopting Spanish-style names and religion. Powell Weaver, an explorer and scout from Tennessee, was one such man. He adopted the name "Paulino" and, with a partner, petitioned Governor Pio Pico for a large land grant in the San Gorgonio Pass.

Eventually, Americans would go to war with Mexico in 1846, defeat them in 1848, and in 1850 set California up as a new state within the United States. All this spelled big changes for the Cahuillas of the San Gorgonio Pass. San Gorgonio Rancho, with its old connections to the San Bernardino Rancho and San Gabriel Mission, became the target of Paulino Weaver's ambitions. This ultimately led to a clash between Weaver and the Cahuillas who originally inhabited the area and needed a domain that was secure from such intrusion.

Weaver's interest in the San Gorgonio Pass went back to the 1830s. It was in the spring of 1832 that he, Kit Carson and Ewing Young first saw the vast pasturelands of San Gorgonio Pass. They had arrived in the Pass from Arizona via the Mohave Trail on their way to Los Angeles. After their long, hot trek across the desert, this area with its small game and rushing streams was a welcome sight and refuge.

While still in Arizona en route to California, these men rode past ancient Indian ruins at Casa Grande on the Gila River. Seeing a high wall at the long-abandoned Indian dwellings, Weaver, an illiterate, part-white, part-Cherokee, Tennessee trapper, asked one of his party to carve "P. Weaver" on it. After he arrived in the San Gorgonio Pass, though impressed with its lush grazing areas, he returned to Arizona several times to trap beavers. There, he also married a Chemehuevi woman.

By 1842, however, Weaver had returned to San Gorgonio Pass and on July 22, 1845 he and Julian (Isaac) Williams petitioned in Spanish to Governor Pio Pico, asking for land that had once been part of San Gabriel Mission. On the petition, Weaver had converted his first name to the Spanish "Paulino." The area that Weaver and Williams wanted covered the southern tip of today's Oak Glen, Cherry Valley, Beaumont and Banning.

This tract of land was not the first one that Weaver had considered. Much earlier, he had been offered land west of San Bernardino, the Rancho Muscupiabe, by the San Gabriel Mission fathers. He turned it down, though, probably because of its exposure to raids by Paiutes who entered the San Bernardino Valley through the Cajon Pass. The land that Weaver and Williams wanted in the San Gorgonio Pass also presented a problem, however: it was already owned. A man named Santiago Johnson had acquired it in 1841 following the secularization of the California missions and sold it that same year to Louis Rubidoux.

In their petition for this land to Governor Pico, Weaver and Williams buttressed their case by claiming to be naturalized Mexican citizens and by assuring the governor that they would "maintain at all times two foreigners for the defense and at the same time protection for the Nation, and moreover, to stock it with five thousand head of cattle." Governor Pico responded to the petition, on September 10, 1845, stating that he would consider their request if Santiago Johnson was cleared of ownership. Without ever receiving any formal grant of ownership to the land from Mexican authorities, Weaver took up residence and continued to claim the land in joint ownership with Williams into the 1850s.

In the last years of Mexican rule in California, Weaver had various dealings with a handful of Americans in San Gorgonio Pass. He also managed to fit in a trip back to Arizona with his old friend, Kit Carson. Around 1845 Weaver was a whip sawyer at a lumbering business (located in today's Edgar Canyon) that was owned by an eccentric named Daniel Sexton. At this time Weaver was living in an old, run-down adobe nearby

Chapter 2–Paulino Weaver and the Cahuillas

that was most likely a structure dating from the 1820s or 1830s on a ranching outpost of the San Gabriel Mission.

While he was living there, he fell seriously ill with rheumatic fever. Fortunately for Weaver, a certain New Englander, Dr. Isaac Smith, and his family happened to be passing through with a wagon train heading west. The kindly doctor cared for him, nursing him back to health. To thank the doctor for having saved him, Weaver insisted that the Smith family stay and he allowed them to establish themselves at the southeast corner of his land in present-day Cherry Valley.

In 1846, Weaver left to go to Arizona with Kit Carson. At Fort Yuma he met General Kearney, who told him to ride to Santa Fe, New Mexico, to guide the Mormon Battalion to Los Angeles. The group consisted of Mormon volunteers who were headed to California on October 19, 1847 to fight the Mexicans on behalf of the United States. When the Mormon group passed through present-day Cherry Valley in 1848, Weaver left them and took up residence, once again, on the property in the Pass that he claimed as his own.

In 1848, the United States took over California from Mexico and Weaver's claim to his land in the Pass was still as shaky as it had been under Mexican rule. Under the new government, many grants were rejected due to lack of accurate measurements and vague identifying landmarks. In the chaos of the late 1840s, Weaver's petition for a grant to the San Gorgonio Rancho was lost. It was not found until after the 1906 San Francisco earthquake.[4]

The land on which Weaver lived had very likely been tilled by Cahuillas long before the arrival of Weaver, since orchards were mentioned in connection with the property in an 1853 report by William Blake, geologist with Lt. Williamson's survey party of the U.S. Corps of Engineers. Weaver's career, with its constant roaming and absences, gives little reason to suppose that he was a farmer or orchard planter. Blake also noted that former occupants of the adobe had been driven away by Indians.

Until sometime in the early 1850s, Weaver's position as one of a small handful of whites in the area was reasonably peaceful. In 1851 he was well-known in the Pass, enough so to be appointed to the Los Angeles grand jury and receive a stipend of ten dollars for his services. He was also employed at Sexton's lumbering business at the rate of twenty-five

---

[4] Dr. Raymond Weaver, Paulino's grandnephew, says no record of this grant ever having been confirmed by the U.S. has been found. A 1949 letter from Dr. Raymond Weaver to Guy Bogart states that Paulino received land near Old Edgar Vineyard for services rendered to California in its fight for independence from Mexico. The property constituted about three acres, on which was the adobe that Weaver used as his home.

cents per day alongside Cahuilla workers from the nearby *rancheria*.

Things were to change for him, however, as relations between whites and Indians flared into open hostility in 1851. In November, Antonio Garra, an Indian leader at Warner Ranch, called a meeting of every leader from the Colorado River to the San Joaquin Valley, a call that included Chemehuevis, Cahuillas, Utes and Utahs. They met at Warner Ranch near Temecula. Garra was gravely concerned about the encroachment of whites into Indian territory in southern California.

From San Diego to Santa Barbara and from far inland to Los Angeles, rampant rumors multiplied the number of Indian warriors into an army of five thousand armed men. Garra fueled the rumors by claiming that Juan Antonio, a powerful Cahuilla leader, was going to double-cross his white friends from San Bernardino to San Gorgonio Pass.

Weaver somehow convinced Juan Antonio to side with the whites, and then hurried to San Bernardino, where he vouched for Juan Antonio's sincerity and loyalty to whites. Juan Antonio also came forward to vow that he would protect the settlers at San Bernardino. Cabazon of Agua Caliente and other Cahuilla leaders also backed away from supporting Garra's plans. In spite of these assurances, the Mormons, who had purchased the San Bernardino Rancho from the Lugos, expected war and hastily constructed a palisaded fort.

Weaver got himself involved in this dispute, yet he chose not to become actively involved in fighting against Garra. For his own safety, he moved from his adobe to shelter at the Asistencia. He told the Mormons that Juan Antonio and twenty-five men were riding off to capture Garra. He had outfitted Juan Antonio with mules and food and encouraged him to capture Garra while he, Weaver, remained at a safe distance.

However, by pitting Juan Antonio and other Indian groups against Garra, Weaver had divided Indian unity and strength. Once Juan Antonio captured Garra, Weaver took on the celebratory task of informing authorities in San Diego and Los Angeles of the capture, thus winning for himself the congratulations that should have been bestowed on Juan Antonio. Once Garra was captured and brought in, Weaver helped Juan Antonio guard Garra at brother Duff Weaver's ranch in San Timoteo Canyon. Not long afterwards, Garra was taken to San Diego, tried and executed. With Garra's execution died the possibility of a unified Indian force that could have repelled whites trespassing on Indian lands.

Although Weaver had been supportive of Juan Antonio in the Garra case, relations with Indians deteriorated afterwards. Soon after the Garra incident, sixty horses in his charge at Yucaipa had been stolen by Indians. A posse of twenty-five men chased the Indians seventy-five miles but could not overtake them. In November 1852 Weaver wrote the *San Francisco*

Chapter 2–Paulino Weaver and the Cahuillas

Herald that the Indians were harassing him by stealing his possessions, killing his animals and even cutting down his peach trees.

Juan Antonio protested that the situation was quite the opposite: Weaver was trespassing on lands that had been granted to the Cahuillas by the recent Treaty of Temecula and he was killing their animals whenever they wandered near his property. On March 31, 1853, the *Daily Alta California* wrote that thirty-two Cahuillas had gone to Indian agent B.D. Wilson in Los Angeles, complaining that Weaver had angered them by shooting their animals and "imposing on them in various ways for sometime past and that, to their repeated protestations, he had paid no regard." Wilson could not help the Cahuillas at all in this case since he was a federal official. Because he did not have jurisdiction in the matter he requested that a justice of the peace in San Bernardino look into the situation. It was probably about this time that Weaver felt it would be wise to sell out soon and leave the area.

Plainly, the relationship between Weaver and Pass Cahuillas that existed at the time of the Garra affair had collapsed. Also, on May 15, 1854 the California Legislature acted to recognize Weaver by awarding him $500 (equal to almost $10,000 in 2010) for the animals and supplies he had given Juan Antonio for his 1851 expedition to capture Garra. (By

A large rock with mortars located on the grounds of the Highland Springs Resort in Cherry Valley. This property once belonged to Dr. Isaac Smith. He bought a large tract of land in the vicinity from Paulino Weaver in a sale that was never valid. Over a thousand Indians gathered on this property for councils as late as the 1850s. This was a time when Americans began moving into traditional Cahuilla territory to squat and take ownership of land and streams.

contrast, Juan Antonio received only cloth, handkerchiefs and sundry items, worth about $100, for his role in Garra's capture.) Now Weaver had some extra financial resources. By December, 1856 Weaver definitely thought that it might be good to leave the Pass forever. So, he sold his remaining land to a man named Soward, signing the document with an

A photo from the early 20th century of the old adobe in Cherry Valley dubbed "The Weaver Adobe." Its walls are no longer standing. Adjacent to this adobe was an old orchard thought to be in existence from the time of the Redlands Asistencia. There was also an Indian *rancheria* here that lasted until the 1850s when the property was bought by the Edgar brothers. Twentieth century observers mistakenly called it a "chapel."

"x." He left his son, Ben, with his brother, Duff, and set off for Arizona.

For years, Paulino Weaver made life miserable for Pass Cahuillas and, then, he left. In Arizona, he did very well, discovering gold on the east bank of the Colorado near La Paz. This find caused a minor gold rush and even the starting of a stagecoach line (the Bradshaw Line) on a trail from Los Angeles to La Paz's gold fields. Weaver, the half-Indian, half-white intruder, luckily sold out when he did and moved to Arizona where he became a revered figure in Arizona history, forever remembered as Prescott, Arizona's First Citizen.

In the meantime, the situation for the Pass Cahuillas did not improve. Around this same time, those who worked for whites in farming and lumbering in the area around Weaver's adobe began to leave and relocate to the Potrero (the heart of today's Morongo Reservation) in Banning. The Cahuillas Weaver left behind faced an uphill battle to find decent land in the Pass that they could call their own forever. Shortly before his departure, Indians under local leaders such as Ajenio in Banning, Juan Antonio in San Timoteo Canyon, and Cabezon of Palm Springs (Agua Caliente) had signed and concluded the Treaty of Temecula in 1852 with the United States. They expected to receive the lands of the San Gorgonio Pass and more land southward to Temecula in exchange for giving up any claim to much broader territories they traditionally occupied and for giving their allegiance to the United States.

However, by the time Paulino Weaver left the San Gorgonio Pass for good in 1856, the United States Senate had still not ratified the Treaty. It turns out that they never did ratify it. From that time until 1892, the situation for the Cahuillas only became more desperate.

Juan Antonio and the Irving Gang

Juan Antonio was already a rising leader among the Cahuilla people when he and his warriors suddenly won great fame in 1851 for tracking down a dangerously armed band of criminals in San Timoteo Canyon and wiping them out with bows and arrows and knives. The gang had come all the way from Los Angeles with the aim of punishing the Lugo family at old San Bernardino. They stole what they could and kidnapped two of Don Antonio Maria del Lugo's grandsons for a $10,000 ransom.

Juan Antonio had been born into the Costo family in the 1780s in a Cahuilla community high in the San Jacinto Mountains. He must have had noticeable leadership qualities at an early point in his life because by the 1820s, the padres of San Gabriel Mission had appointed him to be leader of the San Jacinto Indians. It is possible that he and his followers, including five Mountain Cahuilla clans, were present in San Bernardino in the last years of the Asistencia. Somehow, when the Lugo family won the grant of the entire San Bernardino Rancho, the patriarch of the family, Don Antonio Maria Lugo, befriended Juan Antonio and decided to hire him and his followers to protect the ranch. The Cahuillas took up residence at a spot above the Santa Ana River in today's Colton, a strategic point for defending the ranch against raids by Paiute people who entered the valley through the Cajon Pass.

Juan Antonio provided long, effective guard service for the Lugos and enabled their ranch to flourish. The Lugos raised over ten thousand cattle on the ranch that had once belonged to San Gabriel Mission. Don Antonio, his three sons and nephew and their families prospered. One of his sons, Jose del Carmen Lugo, made his home at the buildings of the old

Asistencia. Other sons had their homes in other parts of the valley.

Unfortunately, in 1851, two of Don Antonio Lugo's grandsons were held in jail in Los Angeles on charges of murder. This caught the attention of an outlaw leader known as John "Red" Irving who had been making lots of trouble in Los Angeles. Irving's gang of thirty ruffians included American rowdies and a bunch of criminals from Australia called "the Sydney Ducks." Town officials seemed powerless to bring Irving and his gang under control. Irving got the idea of bribing Don Antonio Lugo with an offer to forcibly release his grandsons from jail in exchange for $5,000 dollars. Lugo refused the offer and chose to let his grandsons face trial. The trial ended with charges being dropped against the boys. This result enraged Irving.

Arrows from Cahuilla and Serrano bows rained down upon the ill-fated Irving Gang that was trapped in a box canyon in the San Timoteo Canyon. The gang had terrorized Los Angeles, but Juan Antonio and his men wiped it out when they were ordered into action by the Lugo family.

Irving then settled upon a more extreme plan: kidnap the boys and hold them for a ransom of $10,000. In the meantime, the boys had returned to San Bernardino. So, Irving led a detachment of about ten of his gang in that direction, rampaging through the countryside along the way.

When Jose del Carmen Lugo was alerted to the presence of the gang in the area, he went to Major General J.H. Bean for protection from the gang. Bean was in charge of the local American militia, but he was not at his station. A lower level officer turned Lugo down. In desperation, Lugo turned to the faithful employee of the family, Juan Antonio. He later protested to American authorities that he did not realize that Juan Antonio

Chapter 3–Juan Antonio and the Irving Gang

would pursue the task with such thoroughness.

By then, Juan Antonio had had plenty of experience with trouble of this kind. For the past nine years, he had been chasing off or killing cattle and horse thieves from the Mojave Desert. He sprang into action with about twenty of his men armed with knives and bows and arrows and picked up support along the way. He came across the Irving gang who had just broken into one of the Lugo homes near Old San Bernardino. As gang members were making off with expensive horse equipment and other valuables, they fired upon the Cahuillas and the chase began.

The ride out of Rancho San Bernardino, where the plains suddenly led up steep Reservoir Canyon, was grueling. The gang occasionally turned around to fire their Colts at the pursuing Cahuillas, who in turn dismounted at intervals to aim arrows at them. The hundred-yard distance separating the foes was too great for either bullets or bows to inflict fatal harm.

Ascending the crest of Reservoir Canyon, Irving's gang came upon the Sepulveda adobe at Yucaipa. There, they hoped to dismount and refresh themselves and their exhausted horses. Thundering hooves, however, told them that Cahuillas were close on their heels.

Members of the gang wondered if they should remain in place, take a stand and try to rout the Cahuillas before entering the canyon or flee. Irving hastily decided to lead the men onto a logging trail, down Hog Canyon towards San Timoteo Canyon—a decision that proved to be fatal. Serrano people living in the area joined the Cahuillas led by Juan Antonio and swelled their ranks to possibly two hundred warriors. They had the distinct advantage of knowing this landscape well. They urged their horses up the hills above the arroyo, boxed in the gang, and fired upon them from above. Irving, showing his Texas Ranger temperament in battle, rallied his men and fought bravely, until he could no longer sit upright on his horse. He died with five arrow wounds around his heart.

Jose Antonio, *alcalde* [5] and relative of Juan Antonio, was killed in that canyon, and two or three other Indians were wounded. A gang member named Evans, hiding amidst the shrubbery, was the sole survivor from the Irving gang. All the rest were killed and their clothing was stripped off their bodies. Saddles, rifles, pistols, horses, and $5,000 were taken as booty.

As Evans later told the story, he emerged from hiding late that night. In the early dawn, he looked over his friends' corpses and saw that each dead gang member had five to nine arrow wounds. He tramped back to the Lugo rancho, stole a saddled mule, and fled to the Colorado River completely terrified.

---

[5] *alcalde*: a leader or captain.

Chapter 3 – Juan Antonio and the Irving Gang

As soon as he could, Major General Bean rode out to the district at the head of fifty American volunteers. The atmosphere was tense with outraged volunteers eager to teach the Cahuillas a lesson for having killed the white outlaws. Bean reportedly calmed the men and prevented what could have become a bigger battle with the Indians. Nevertheless, he reprimanded Juan Antonio for killing white men, even though they were criminals. The Cahuillas must have been surprised by the whites' reaction, since they had simply performed their expected duty, as they had for years, working for the Lugos. Within days, Juan Antonio and his band fled eastward to the hills of the San Gorgonio Pass, perhaps under orders from General Bean.

L.A. County Attorney, Benjamin Hayes came to San Bernardino, investigated the affair and found the Cahuillas not guilty. A coroner's inquest further absolved Juan Antonio of all guilt. *The Los Angeles Star* of 14 June 1851 said: "…he (Juan Antonio) is hereby notified that he can return with his people to their homes…with a guaranty that no harm shall be done him…." Out of gratitude, Judge Hayes awarded Juan Antonio $100 worth of cloth, hats, and handkerchiefs paid for out of the Los Angeles County treasury. The Cahuillas were coaxed into returning to work for the Lugos and once again settled at Politana (today's Colton). Lugo lost $2,000 in clothing, saddles, tack and equipment the Irving gang had stolen from his ranch. It was probably very irksome to him that only one pair of his pants (*pantalones*) were recovered from the grand theft. One can imagine his dismay at losing his pants in this dramatic episode. The excitement of the affair was too much for Lugo and soon afterwards he decided to sell Rancho San Bernardino and move his herds to properties closer to Los Angeles.

The incident immediately put the Cahuillas and the San Gorgonio Pass "on the map." It underlined the urgency to do something to secure a homeland for the southern California Indians. Within a short time, Americans proposed several treaties with the Cahuillas.

In the aftermath of the destruction of Irving and his gang, the knowledge that Juan Antonio and his men, armed only with bows and arrows, had nearly wiped out a heavily armed criminal gang of white men shocked Los Angeles and coastal communities as far away as San Francisco. His status, both among his Cahuilla followers and the whites of southern California, rose dramatically. Within a short time, he would be instrumental in putting down a widespread Indian revolt in the area and be the first of many leaders to sign a treaty with the federal government.

Juan Antonio and the Treaty of Temecula

Juan Antonio was summoned by U.S. agent Oliver Wozencraft to appear in Temecula on January 4, 1852, but Juan Antonio was wary of the invitation. The occasion was the signing of a treaty that was presented to the Indian groups of southern California. It was intended to secure a large tract of land about thirty miles by forty miles in size as a reservation for them. Juan Antonio's presence was important to agent Wozencraft because of the reputation he and the Cahuilla people had gained from crushing the dreaded Irving gang during the summer of 1851. His reputation since that event had only grown greater because of his role in undermining the Indian revolt that started at Warner Springs. There, a rival leader named Antonio Garra led a movement to drive whites out of southern California completely. Juan Antonio intervened as a friend of the whites and managed to capture Garra and hand him over to white authorities. When Garra was later executed in San Diego, the threat of a widespread Indian rebellion in southern California was ended forever and Juan Antonio also disposed of a potential rival. Naturally, the Americans, therefore, felt that Juan Antonio's presence was important for a successful conclusion to the treaty process.

Juan Antonio was on edge about coming to Temecula to sign the treaty since there were Luiseños there and it was hostile territory for Cahuillas. The Luiseños had not forgiven or forgotten the massacre of more than fifty of their men in a clash with the Cahuillas led by Juan Antonio five years earlier. Another Cahuilla leader, Ajenio of the village of Piatopa, in today's Banning Water Canyon, was also nervous about the prospect of an ugly incident in Temecula. He left his village for Temecula to the weeping and wailing of village women who thought they might not see him return alive.

Chapter 4–Juan Antonio and the Treaty of Temecula

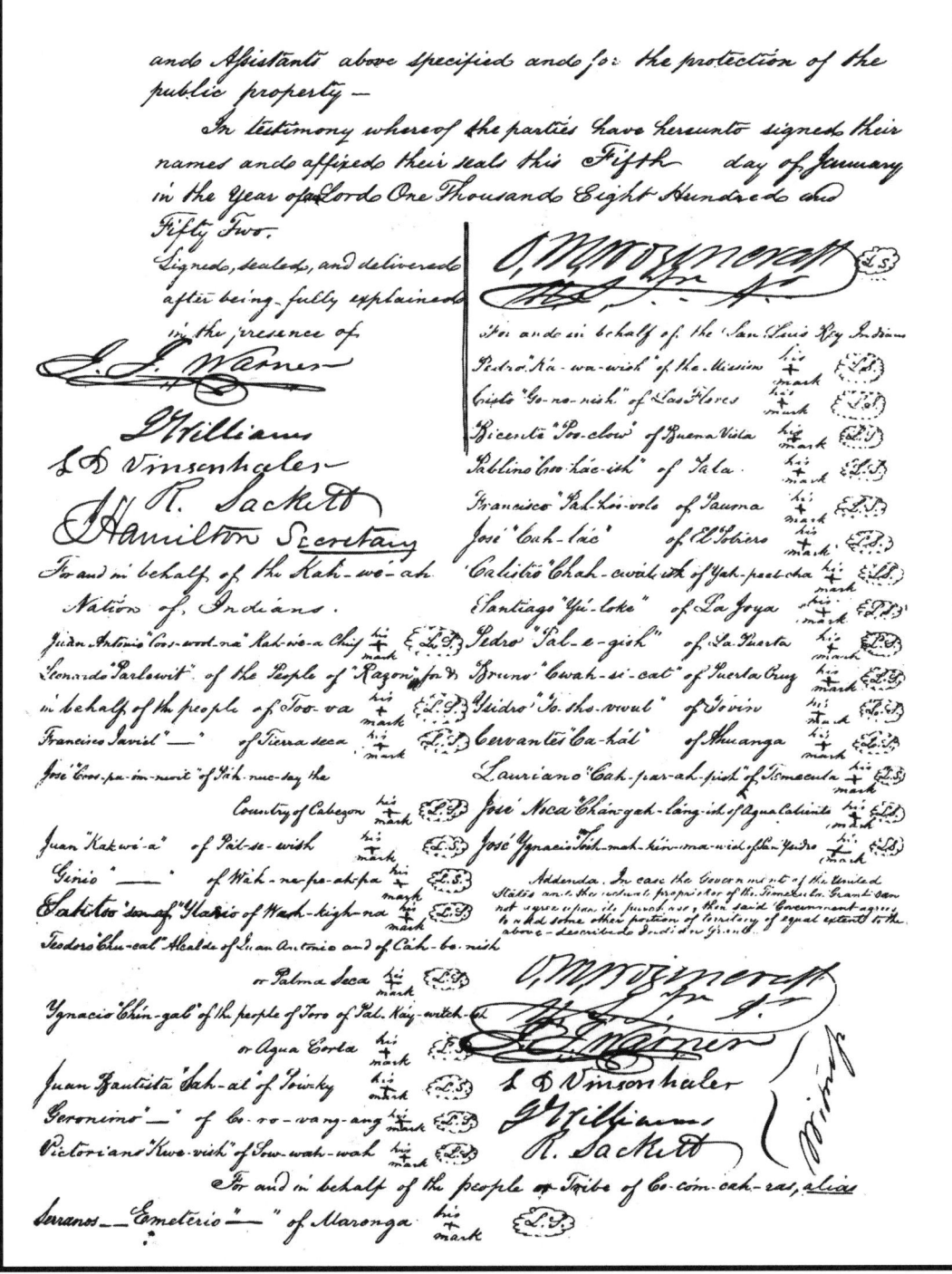

This is the signature page of the Treaty of Temecula concluded at Temecula in January 1852 by Oliver Wozencraft representing the U.S. Government. Many leaders of the Cahuilla, Luiseño and Cocomaricopa villages attended. Juan Antonio was the first Indian to put his mark to the document. It was never ratified, but instead, was "lost" and did not come to light until decades later. In the meantime, the Indians continued to lose their farms and even the crops in the ground, team animals, and water ditches to unscrupulous American squatters.

Chapter 4 – Juan Antonio and the Treaty of Temecula

Juan Antonio was also possibly irked by the insult he had received earlier from the Americans. On a hot, dry, summer day in 1851 he had journeyed from San Bernardino Valley to Chino to await the arrival of U.S. agent George Barbour. The purpose of the appointment was, as it was on this occasion, to sign a treaty of peace with the U.S. government that would grant his people a permanent homeland and a variety of other benefits. He waited five days, in mounting anger, for U.S. agent Barbour to arrive. After the fifth day, Juan Antonio's patience wore out and he left for Politana, his village above the banks of the Santa Ana River, in today's Colton. Later, he learned that Barbour had been trying to put down Indian uprisings in Tulare County and could not come down to Chino at the appointed time. Months passed and, finally, he and other leaders of southern California's Cahuilla, Cocomaricopa and Luiseño communities received the summons to gather at Temecula. Wozencraft's messenger had been firm that this was an order, not a request, and punishment would follow if Cahuilla leaders did not appear.

As Juan Antonio rode to Temecula, he was also possibly thinking back to the summer before when a large Mormon contingency had arrived from Utah and purchased the San Bernardino Rancho from the Lugo family. They had asked Juan Antonio and his people to leave Politana. The Cahuillas then relocated to a place called Sahatapa, far up in the San Timoteo Canyon, not far from the summit of the San Gorgonio Pass. The relocation, in all probability, had taken place in the latter half of 1851 and made Juan Antonio keenly aware of the need for U.S. protection and guarantee of lands for Cahuilla people.

On January 4, 1852, having ridden on horseback from Sahatapa with mixed feelings, Juan Antonio, Juan Bautista, and their retinue of bodyguards, appeared in Temecula. The atmosphere must have been charged with tension as Juan Antonio and the other Cahuilla leaders arrived at the ranch of Pablo Apis. Wozencraft succeeded in keeping the situation calm among the groups assembled. He brought out a document for the leaders to sign with their marks. The document, a treaty, held the promise of a large inland sanctuary for them.

The treaty they were about to sign, the Treaty of Temecula, was only one of eighteen treaties currently being negotiated with California Indians throughout the state. These so-called Eighteen Treaties promised to set aside 8,500,000 acres for reservations in exchange for the Indians' giving up claims to 75,000,000 acres of California lands that were once their domains.

The Treaty of Temecula, like the other seventeen treaties, was an outgrowth of the Treaty of Guadalupe Hidalgo that the U.S. had concluded with Mexico when it won its war with Mexico and control of what was to become the American Southwest. On September 9, 1850 Alta California became the State of California and the seventy-year reign of the Spanish and

Chapter 4–Juan Antonio and the Treaty of Temecula

the Mexicans in California came to a close. American authorities were then expected to hammer out arrangements with the indigenous people and with former Mexican nationals.

By the terms of the Treaty of Guadalupe Hidalgo, especially Articles VIII and XI, the American government was supposed to protect Indian ownership of lands and not place burdens on them to relocate. In reality, Indians often found themselves pushed out by American settlers arriving in great numbers during the Gold Rush of 1848. American settlers coming to California were hungry for land and the new government of California usually favored them when land claims were being filed. The Treaty of Guadalupe Hidalgo had also promised California Indians all the rights of U.S. citizens, but these provisions were ignored.

The terms of the Treaty of Temecula must have looked acceptable to the people attending the January 4th ceremony. Its clauses set aside a large inland reservation for the Indians of southern California. Article III of the treaty defined the boundaries of the reservation to include land that covered the area from San Gorgonio Pass to Warner's ranch, an area of roughly 1,200 square miles. It was intended for the sole use of the Indians. Annual allotments of food, supplies and tools were also provided for in this treaty under other articles. Few whites lived in this area, so the treaty appeared workable. The Indian leaders signed with their marks of "x" and felt satisfied that in signing, they had won security for their people. They left to return to their villages the following day, January 5, 1852.

What Juan Antonio and the other Indian leaders could not have known, however, was that there was already a scheme afoot in the California State legislature to produce a law that would favor white squatters' claims to lands of the Indians and Mexicans. The California legislature passed such a law in April 1852. This law, the California Possessory Claim Act, required that property owners file written documents as evidence of their ownership. Even Juan Antonio, knowledgeable in many foreign ways, did not have an understanding of the process of securing land ownership by submitting legal documents. The California legislature also passed an Act for the Government and Protection of the Indians that stripped the Indians of any right to testify in court to protect their interests and allowed white squatters access to getting ownership of Indian lands. To make matters worse, the federal government passed an "Act to Ascertain and Settle Private Claims in the State of California (the "Gwin Act"). This law required land claimants to appear before the Land Commission in San Francisco to secure their land titles by 1853. All these laws had the effect of undermining the claims of California Indians to their lands. Juan Antonio, Ajenio and Cabezon would soon feel the effects of these laws, as whites settled on Cahuilla lands, piece by piece, from San Timoteo Canyon to Whitewater. California law, as noted, prevented the Cahuillas from

Chapter 4–Juan Antonio and the Treaty of Temecula

fighting back and challenging the claims of others.

How could this happen when Juan Antonio and other Cahuilla, Luiseño and Cocomaricopa Indians had just signed an important treaty with U.S. Agent Wozencraft? The answer is that the U.S. Senate failed to approve the Eighteen Treaties and the Indians were not informed of the Senate's refusal to approve them.

Lawmakers in the California State legislature had fought hard to prevent the U.S. Congress from approving the new treaties with the California Indians. The California delegation to the U.S. Congress put up a fierce struggle against the Eighteen Treaties. In the end, the U.S. Senate, under President Fillmore, refused to ratify any of the Eighteen Treaties with the California Indians. Their brief, cruel words stated: "Resolved. That the Senate does not advise and consent to the ratification of the treaty of peace and friendship made and concluded at the village of Temecula, California, between the United States Indian agent, O.M. Wozencraft, of the one part, and the captains and head men of the following nations viz., The nation of San Luis Rey Indians, the Kah-we-as, and the tribe of Co-Com-Cah-ras (Cocomaricopas), of the other part...." The Senate did the same with the other seventeen California nations of Indians.

The vote was done in a secret executive session and the documents were hidden away in a secret file. Juan Antonio could be forgiven if he returned to his village at Sahatapa, believing that he and his people were secure in their lands and free to farm, hunt, and raise their families in peace. He had staked his career on a policy of cooperation with the Americans and believed that soon his people could safely occupy the lands newly set aside for them. He also expected the quick arrival of supplies of food, tools, animals, and teachers promised by other terms of the treaty. No one seems to have ever told him that the Treaty was worthless and that the new government of California had worked against ratification.

Within one or two years, white squatters began crowding the Cahuillas near their farms and villages at Akavat, Sahatapa, Piatopa and Bonopiapa. Too late, Juan Antonio and his people must have realized that the lands promised by the Treaty would never become theirs nor would they receive any of the supplies of farming tools and animals that they needed to survive.

The Eighteen Treaties, including the Treaty of Temecula, unbelievably, were lost for half a century and were only rediscovered by accident in 1905. The Eighteen Treaties have also been called "the lost treaties," and that name fits the picture in another sense: because of those "lost" treaties, the Indians of California lost all but a very small fraction of their traditional lands, never to be reclaimed.

5

The Case of *John Morongo et al vs. John North et al*

For a long time after the failure of the Treaty of Temecula, the Cahuilla people of the San Gorgonio Pass continued to yield ground to American squatters. From the 1850s through the 1880s more and more Americans came to the area and saw that there were large tracts of apparently unoccupied land that they thought were going to waste. In reality there were fewer Cahuilla people in the Pass than there were at the beginning of the century. Decades of white intrusion into Cahuilla territory had been the cause of their constant dislocation and their dwindling numbers. In the squatters' way of thinking, however, the unoccupied spaces were "wasteland" that they could put to better use. It seemed to invite them to squat on the land, especially on the best parcels located near the streams that flow down from the San Bernardino Mountains onto the broad plains of the Pass.

By mid-century, the Cahuillas had abandoned their villages at Guachama, in the San Timoteo Canyon and in the Pass all the way to Whitewater, except for the Potrero *rancheria* northeast of today's city of Banning. Newcomers gained legal title to the lands and streams all throughout the Pass and began building the communities of Beaumont, Banning and Cherry Valley. Even at the Potrero *rancheria*, though, the Cahuillas were not secure. Squatters harassed them there as well. There was no place in all the San Gorgonio Pass, it seemed, that was legally theirs. President Ulysses. S. Grant, however, took a first step to correct this situation by creating a number of reservations for southern California Indians, including the Potrero, or Morongo Reservation on May 15, 1876. On August 25, 1877 President Rutherford B. Hayes expanded upon Grant's executive order by adding more acreage to the reservation.

Both executive orders, however, had a fatal flaw: by mistake, they

Chapter 5–The case of John Morongo et al vs. John North et al

excluded Section 36 from being included in the reservation. This section was vital to the Potrero because of the stream, the pastures, the agricultural fields and the Cahuilla village it contained. A number of investors from outside the area noticed the omission and tried to win control of the section from the Indians. This alarmed the U.S. Agent and the U.S. Government finally became convinced of the need to save the areas set aside for the Indians, especially Section 36, since it was one of the last remaining tracts of land in southern California that were any good. To secure it for the Cahuilla people meant, however, that the U.S. Government would have to remove squatters and pay off two influential businessmen, John North and Richard Gird, who had filed a lawsuit on November 5, 1887 against John Morongo, the acting leader of the Cahuillas, to win title to Section 36. Later that month the case was removed from the jurisdiction of San Bernardino County and was transferred to the U.S. Circuit Court In Los Angeles.

The following year, the Cahuillas and their lawyers moved into action and filed a countersuit against North and Gird at the same court in Los Angeles. It got the attention of Judge Erskine who made an important decision. He ordered the case filed by North and Gird to be put on hold until the rights of the Cahuillas to the disputed lands could be first determined.

Attorney George Otis represented North and Gird in their lawsuit, while Shirley C. Ward and Indian Agent Colonel Preston represented John Morongo and the Cahuilla people at the Potrero in their case which was known as CC 89 *John Morongo et al vs. John G. North et al.*[6] This case was allowed to proceed first, ahead of North and Gird's lawsuit.

At the first session of the trial held at Banning U.S. Master in Chancery, Charles L. Batcheller, called many Indians who had lived for years at the Potrero to testify. As he surveyed the crowded room, he probably felt uneasy about this case. Local Cahuillas would be testifying in their native language. The agreed-upon procedure would be cumbersome and slow: Cahuilla testimony would be translated into Spanish, then from Spanish to English by Frank Smith, son of pioneer Dr. Isaac Smith. (The Smiths had an interest in the outcome of the case because they had expanded their holdings in the Pass by obtaining lands once intensively utilized by the Cahuillas.)

Batcheller had made a tiring trip from Los Angeles to Banning and may well have wondered how long the case would last. On one side of the room were Indian Agent Colonel Preston; Ward, the Indians' attorney; and the

---

[6] The other plaintiffs named in the case were Rafael Morongo, Francisco Morongo, Tomas Morongo, Jose Chino, Pablo Gabriel, Juan Lugo, Juan Gabriel, Jose Gabriel, Ajunio Gabriel, Duarte Gabriel, Felipe Alapasio, Jurupa Ventura, Louis Ventura, Juan Duarte, Jose Duarte, Arguello Lugo, Jose Romero, and Tomas Cisco (all residents of the County of San Bernardino). CC 89 John Morongo et al vs. John G. North et al. National Archives and Records Administration, Laguna Niguel. RG 21, Records of the District Courts of the United States, Southern Division, Civil Case files 1887-1912, Box # 18.

Chapter 5–The case of John Morongo et al vs. John North et al

Stick and thatch home on Morongo Reservation around 1886.

plaintiff, John Morongo. On the opposite side, were John North and attorney Otis. Translator Frank Smith was nearby in order to be able to hear all of the testimony and render translations. At stake was the Banning Potrero, which was the very last parcel of decent land in the Pass that Cahuillas occupied. If they lost the case, they would be evicted entirely from their ancestral lands in the Pass. Numerous witnesses were called and testimony began on a Tuesday in April, 1889.

On April 4, a week before the trial, Ward and Agent Preston had ridden half a day from San Bernardino to the Potrero to inspect the claims filed by North and Gird. They must have realized the extreme danger that these two businessmen from Riverside and Chino posed for Pass Cahuillas and the U.S. Government's plan for a reservation. An article in the *San Bernardino Times Index* praised the "sterling character" of Mr. Gird, but Ward and Preston knew that neither he nor North had charity in their heart for the Cahuilla people. Only three years earlier, they had Cahuillas removed from a parcel of land they occupied at Potrero.

During the trial, Ward attempted to bring out proof of the Cahuillas' long occupation of the Potrero. For this purpose, he had asked Captain John Morongo to round up credible witnesses who could prove that important point.

The first witness sworn in was John Morongo himself, a middle-aged, stocky Indian dressed in western suit and string tie, sporting a neat haircut parted on the left. A reporter for the local newspaper, *The Banning Herald,* noted

Chapter 5–The case of John Morongo et al vs. John North et al

John Morongo was the plaintiff in one of two cases involving interloping businessmen, John North and partner, Richard Gird. Those men had tried to win control of the vital Section 36 at the Potrero. Eventually, the settlement arranged by the Smiley Commission brought an end to the cases.

that Morongo spoke "proper" English as he recalled the Potrero from his childhood. His people cultivated the lower reservation land and pastured stock on the upper areas, he said. Truthfully he could not recall the size of the village from the days of his childhood.

Between courtroom preliminaries and protocol and Morongo's well-spoken testimony, it was afternoon before Antonio Ajenio of Piatopas gave his testimony. A reporter for the local newspaper recounted that during the questioning Ajenio sat with the dignity of a senator. His face registered dignity, but he must have been tense and apprehensive about the outcome of the case for his people. The last time he had attended such an important ceremony with white men had been at Temecula over thirty-five years earlier to sign a treaty handed to him by U.S. Agent Oliver Wozencraft.

Ajenio must have been keenly aware of the promise that was made at that time for a large secure reservation—a promise that had never been kept. The situation for the Cahuillas had only grown more desperate during those decades and Ajenio probably dreaded another catastrophic setback for his people.

The newspaper reporter observing the trial made it a point to say that the Cahuilla witnesses could not state their age or the duration of their residence at Potrero, in years. It appears that the witnesses were nervous and unprepared to give answers in the manner whites would. In contrast, for instance, white witnesses often cited the exact year they first observed Cahuillas at Potrero. This disparity was not caused by a simple lapse of memory by the Cahuillas, for they knew their history, their origins, their creation stories and all aspects of their culture and could repeat them with great feats of memory that required days of unceasing recitation. The contrast in the courtroom was that of cultural difference.

When questioned by attorney Ward, the elderly Ajenio did not "know" his age. Ajenio reiterated many times that the land had always belonged to his people. Even when Ward wished to move him on to other questions, such as, how long the Cahuilla people had used the pastures at the Potrero, Ajenio repeated, "We have always used the upper *cienaga* for our horses." Ward knew that the repetition of "we have always been here" would not advance the case and ended his questioning of Ajenio. The Cahuilla leader, obviously despondent and flustered, was dismissed.

Spanish-speaking Juan Tomato was sworn in. Handsome and well dressed, he could not give information on early Indian development on Potrero, since he had come to the area as a grownup. When questioned by Ward, he recalled Indians using land north of the Jost homestead for pasturing their stock before any whites were there. He recalled Mrs. Toutain coming to the Potrero after an American sheep herder, Chapin, had rented Potrero land in the 1850s.

Duarte Gabrielle, the next witness, testified that barley, alfalfa, beans, corn, pumpkins and watermelons were among the crops the Indians grew. Next, Hosea Chino, praised by the press for his distinguished good looks and curly hair, verified what previous witnesses had said, that Indians had used the upper Potrero as a horse pasture, but without giving dates.

Following his testimony, the court recessed until Wednesday, when the remaining pro-Indian witnesses were to be examined. When the trial resumed, solemn Francisco Morongo took the stand. He answered forcefully that the Indians had been on the Potrero for a long time, but like the others, he could not cite dates. Next, nervous Captain Pablo took the oath. He had been born at Potrero and had lived there since, although he could not remember dates when pressed. Since he was agitated, Ward did not question him further. Clearly, when Cahuilla witnesses testified, they were on edge and seemingly bewildered in the matter of dates.

Attorney Ward was well aware of events that had precipitated this trial. For decades prior, whites had settled on Indian lands surrounding the Potrero. Some claimed they had been squatters prior to the formation of the reservation and others lamely claimed that the Indians were not making use of some of the land, so they simply took the land they wanted and claimed they were making good use of it. Not even the executive orders of two presidents were enough to keep them from encroaching on lands set aside for the Cahuillas. John G. North and Richard Gird were only the latest of the newcomers but they were the boldest in claiming Potrero land and water for themselves. Ward was determined to fight even more fiercely for the Indians' cause.

Chapter 5–The case of John Morongo et al vs. John North et al

Ironically, it was the white witnesses whose testimony often supplied those dates that confirmed the claims of the Cahuillas as to how long they lived at the Potrero. The first witness when the trial moved to San Bernardino was Newton Noble, who stated that Indians had cattle, horses, and mules at the Potrero in 1853. Ten years later, he started renting pasture on Indian land. Seventy-six-year old James W. Waters, Sr. testified next that when he first became aware of Ajenio Potrero in 1864, Indians were then at the mouth of the Potrero then. Spaniard Perfecto Albillar followed, testifying that Indians were using the Potrero in 1851. James Banks of Temecula recalled forty or fifty houses at Potrero in 1860 and also recalled one of the white squatters living at Potrero in 1874, many years after the Indians had set up their village there. William H. Fellows, the next witness, was first aware of Potrero Village in 1856, and at that date Indians were already farming at Potrero and keeping their horses above the area. He stated under oath that there were no whites at Potrero then.

The next witness packed the courtroom and lent a bit of humor to the dour hearing. Daniel Sexton, who had lumbered in Edgar Canyon in the early 1840s with Paulino Weaver, took the stand and made the most vivid impressions on his audience in the San Bernardino County courtroom. First, he estimated that 1,500 Indians were at the Potrero when he first went there. He emphasized that they had plows, hoes, other farming implements as well as blacksmiths who could make and repair metal tools. However, what the court audience had been waiting for from Sexton, it got next. He related with relish his stories about fighting multiple bears in Edgar Canyon, a large 4th of July celebration to which Indians had been invited, and other frontier-type stories. In spite of his probably exaggerated tales of battles with grizzly bears, he did leave the audience with the knowledge that over 1,000 Indians were living at Potrero long before whites had squatted there.

Less entertaining, Ransome Moore followed, citing that Indians had stock in upper Potrero in 1864 and claimed the area, but he stated that he and others also had cattle there.

Frank Smith, son of Pass pioneer Dr. Isaac Smith, was eight when his family moved to San Gorgonio Pass. His father had aided an ailing Paulino Weaver. His testimony placed Indians at Potrero in 1855. He recalled that they had transported grapevines from Weaver's land to Potrero. He remembered that Chief Ajenio moved to the Potrero in 1855 or 1856 and that Captain Pablo was there around 1860. His testimony, in an indirect manner, confirmed what Sexton said about the numbers of Cahuillas in the region. He recalled from his childhood days council gatherings of over 1,000 Cahuillas on his father's ranch at Highland Springs.

Rosa Sansavine Noble, wife of Newt Noble, was the last to testify before this important case was transferred yet again. A noted beauty, she took the stand and in her testimony confirmed the early existence of a large Indian community at the Potrero.

At this point, Attorney Ward focused his thoughts on the next stage of the case to be held, at his request, at the Ninth Circuit Court of the United States, Southern District of California, in Los Angeles. Witnesses had to be subpoenaed for deposition to Mr. Batcheller's office over the Farmers' and Merchants' Bank on the southeast corner of Main and Commercial Streets in Los Angeles. Ward's defense of the Indian cause would be based on the relevance of the Treaty of Guadalupe Hidalgo to the Cahuillas' rights to the parcel at the Potrero. He would argue forcefully that the Cahuillas were certainly part of the old Mission system and therefore entitled to the protection of their lands under the provisions of the treaty. It was important to the success of the case that the Cahuillas make the long journey to Los Angeles from the Pass to testify. (Unfortunately, we cannot share what witnesses actually testified in Los Angeles since only procedural aspects of the case seem to have survived.)

Throughout this time, all parties were in a state of high tension since much was at stake. In the end, both the case of North and Gird against John Morongo and Morongo's case against them were closed after an important federal commission was empowered to investigate the increasingly desperate situation for all southern California Mission Indians. This commission, known as the Smiley Commission, reached its conclusions in the last days of 1891 and recommended the creation of reservations with secure boundaries. President William H. Harrison approved the Smiley Commission recommendations on December 29, 1891.

Smiley Commission recommendations led to a re-designed Morongo reservation that was forever secure from intrusion by squatters and unscrupulous men like North and Gird. The basic solution to resolve the complex issues involved here was to change the checkerboard pattern of the Morongo reservation and to group all the Cahuilla lands into a more compact form northeast of the town of Banning. Squatters gave up their claims of Cahuilla lands and water at the Potrero and were given acreage in the middle of the Pass on either side of the railroad in return. The Banning Water Canyon was taken from the Cahuillas in exchange for another section from the railroad. The Southern Pacific railroad got other parcels in compensation for the sections they yielded to the Cahuillas. Some of the land in the Banning watershed that was taken from the tribe remained in the control of the U.S. Forest Service. The vitally important water, pastures, agricultural land and Section 36 at the Potrero were preserved for the Cahuillas.

Banning today would look very different had these exchanges not

Chapter 5–The case of John Morongo et al vs. John North et al

taken place. The western boundary of the reservation would have been at San Gorgonio Avenue, for instance, and parcels of Indian land would have been interspersed with white-owned lands in checkerboard fashion much the way Palm Springs is today.

The lawsuits of the parties, John Morongo on the one hand and John North and Richard Gird on the other, lent much urgency to the Smiley Commission's efforts to work out a settlement before it was too late.

On December 14, 1908, about one hundred years after Spanish influence had penetrated the Pass and sixteen years after the North Gird trial ended, a patent was issued to the Morongo band of Mission Indians for the lands recommended by the Smiley Commission. The Commission's work thus eventually secured a permanent home for the Pass Cahuillas and ended a tragic ordeal of dislocation that had lasted from 1842 to 1892.